Starg

Born in Lancashire, Robert Hull taught English for over 25 years, first in Canada then in the UK, and has written two much-praised books on teaching. Now, though in demand as a creative writing teacher and highly respected reviewer and anthologist, Robert devotes much of his time to writing. The main inspirations for his fine poetry and magical stories are travel, a special interest in ancient culture, myth and folklore, and everyday life in modern Sussex, where he and his wife, Jan, have their home.

*Poet talking about his poem written on recycled paper helping . . . ,
Last Mile of a Holiday, Froglet,* and *Galileo's Story* were first published
in Green Poetry, Sea Poetry, Poems for Summer, and Science Poetry
respectively (Wayland). *On television tonight* was first published in Can
you hear? (Piper).

Edited by Vic Parker
Designed by Diane Thistlethwaite

Published by Hodder Children's Books 1997

10 9 8 7 6 5 4 3 2 1

ISBN 0340 69348 7

Printed and bound in Great Britain by Clays ltd, St Ives plc

Hodder Children's Books
A division of Hodder Headline plc
338 Euston Road
London NW1 3BH

Stargrazer

poems by
Robert Hull

illustrations by Peter Bailey

Hodder
Children's
Books

a division of Hodder Headline plc

Contents

Poet talking about his poem written on recycled paper helping . . .

I'm writing this on re-
cycled paper, 'Helping to use
the Earth's resources economically',
it says

in nice brown ink under a green
tree on the back
of the exercise-book
I write poems in.

I suppose it's alright to write
if we don't use
too much paper and chop down
too many of you, trees,

so I've started to write poems
with the fewest words I can in
though even in this one
perhaps I could have written less (sorry,

fewer) words and crossed out some.
But, in future, trees,
I'll be writing economicaller
stories and poems (see? 'economicaller'

's shorter than 'more economical' – and
comicaller) and if they keep on dwindling
like rainforests and ice-fields
I'll soon be an Earth-preserving

sort of writer writing hardly anything,
which could be a good thing
– for the environment I mean.
(I'd written all this down

last night then suddenly
in my dream this falling
tree
yells, *'Who are you kidding,*

just who
do
you
think you're kidding?')

Tarasque

*Legend says that the Tarasque was a monster who
came from Asia to live at Avignon in the River Rhone,
devouring anything that passed near its banks. Sixteen
men went out to fight it but were burnt up by its breath.
St Martha finally confronted it, calmed it, and having
sprinkled it with holy water, brought it back on a lead
to Tarascon, where it eventually died. A swimming,
moving model of the Tarasque now 'lives' in the
moat of the castle at Tarascon.*

It's raining.
Traffic throws up thick spray,
and water trickles down the bark
of the plane trees.

Bubbles mark the spot
where he'll surface.

Moat-water sluicing over metal molars
the fanged face rises
for the nth time this morning
wearily.

A slow swirl of missile-like tail-fin,
a heavy heave round of rust-coloured flank,
a blink down of lazy brown metal eyelid
like an old car headlamp slowly.

Everything done deliberately
as if all his battery were failing.
He settles low in the water
that foams and seethes round him
till he's lying there quiet
as if still in wait.

He hisses a little
through the portholes of his nostrils,
arches his plated back like a fairground ride,
lifts a dripping jaw like a drawbridge
and lets it drop back.

No looping coil of fire
snaking out to lassoo late shepherds anymore.
He's flameless.
No single flicker along the teeth.

He plunges his head down forward
like a locomotive taking a bath
slowly subsides himself back under
with a sigh of water
and disappears.

Bubbles mark the spot.

None of the wagon-drivers
or sheltering tourists
seem to have noticed.

But he's gone,
as if drowned
weighted down
with disillusion –
a choked moat
an unravenous routine
and centuries of rain.

No crunchy cartfuls of pilgrims,
and this modern traffic
is inedible.

No one throws him maidens,
only old prams.

Maths person

'Maths gets everywhere,'
he used to say.
'Observe things.'

'Look at me for instance,
notice the **spheroidal**
bald bonce, the nose
fit for a **hypotenuse**,
the **parabolas**
of the bushy eyebrows.
And the clothes.
Which bit of gear's
a **rectangle**
with a **trapezium**
on each end? Clue – yellow
with blue spots. Like it? No?
Well bow-ties
are worn daft this year.
Note the **symmetrical**
glasses, the **a-
symmetrical**

face. Observe
the trousers' nearly **parallel**
creases and behind as I **rotate**
through **180 degrees**,
the **intersecting**
cool braces in red
with nattily **adjacent**
and also **opposite**
angles. Spot
the **elliptical**
hole in the right sock.'

Lesson over. Spheroidal
head gleaming, he walks a straight
shortest-distance-between-two-points
down the corridor, the elliptical
hole in the right sock
winking at us.
We notice this year
shoe-heels are worn
nearly triangular.

Last mile of a holiday

We watched the town
fall back behind the cliff
and felt the boat
start to lift and dip.

We raised binoculars
at passing beaches
and bays where nothing
seemed to be happening.

Two hours slid by
of only islands
and cliffs and flying
fish making quick

twenty-yard dashes
away from us leaving
grooves of dark
on the swaying stillness.

The boat was already
nearing harbour
when we heard the cry –
'Dolphins!'

And there! A dark fin
in a fold of the wake
and a face nosing up spray
like a submarine

from just under the surface –
a kind of grin
where its mouth was –
then a dozen or so more

up ahead, not chasing,
their slow
black fins following
each other over

in a continuous
revolving movement
like the teeth of a huge
saw. It was the still,

blue sun-filled
old sea simply
showing us
why we came.

A full day in the life of a king

Edward 7 woke up with a busy day ahead starting as
                usual with breakfast including
poached eggs haddock bacon mushrooms kidneys
                chicken raspberries

Followed by a fine morning shooting *pheasant woodcock*
                grouse duck ptarmigan
                as usual

Followed by returning for lunch with twelve courses
                as usual including
soup quail whiting grouse woodcock ptarmigan partridge
                trout truffles sorbets

Followed by racing at Ascot closely pursued by *tea with*
                pâté and crumpets

Followed by the opera at Covent Garden including
                from 8.30 to 9.30
interval refreshments prepared by six footmen with
                tablecloths silver and gold plate
and a dozen hampers containing ten cold courses
                consisting of as usual
consommé lobster sole duck leveret lamb plovers'
                eggs pigeon chicken
tongue and ham jelly oysters sandwiches desserts
                patisseries

Followed by Acts 4 and 5 and the applause
and the curtain coming down at last and the
                              royal coach leaving
with His Royal Highness Edward 7
containing His Royal Highness's royal interior
containing a large selection of *trout toast woodcock*
                              lobster patisseries plovers' eggs
bacon oysters pheasant haddock duck sorbets solos
                              duets cigar-smoke champagne

All shaken up together in the royal interior in the
                              royal coach
swaying slowly back to the palace

Where the king went to sleep with a small *plate of*
                              sandwiches by the bed
in case he got hungry as usual during the night

And so another full day came to an end
followed by next morning when Edward 7 woke up as
                              usual with a busy day ahead

Riddles

I snap at early light.
I spit in whispers like polite fat.
I pour like scratchy sand.
I swirl, I drown.
I'm taken off into the dark.

(a cornflake)

I unlock walls.
I examine possessions.
I return with permissions
and refusals.

(credit card)

I'm crushed against white walls.
I creak against my own shadow.
I wander crazily,
leaving behind me
a trail of dark.

(pen)

Here I lie.
Once I was up high.
Now I'm not.
And I've lost my little pot.

(acorn)

Shadows

Lovely the shadows
of gulls at rest on the water

of trout hovering over sunlit gravel
in the river

of the oak at sunset
lengthening down the hill.

Different the shadows

that darken the chart

fill the window

stop the heart.

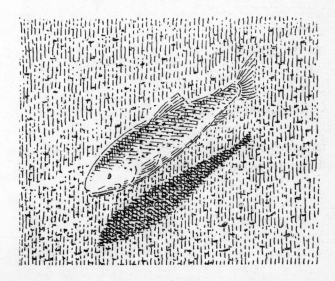

Vinandr's Mere

Vinandr's Mere is possibly what the ancient
Norse warriors called the largest lake in the Lake
District, Windermere.

Invading dark
near 3 o'clock. From its flank,

lightning's axe
smashes to the fell,

cleaving the long mere
to the bone.

Behind tall driving rain
painted snarl of carved prows

silenced,
muffled splashings

of hurled anchor.
Coming ashore,

famished blades
that draw blood from the wind.

In ash trees along the Brathay
swoosh of hauled oars,

the river brimming brown foam;
spearing wind, hiss of reeds,

clatter of gear in birches, voices.
Coiling mists fall back,

a lance of last sun
glimmers against crags,

their round helms glistening.
Then murk, then dark.

By drowned day,
new quiet.

Across the fells are scattered
discarded shields.

Self-advert for mole programme tonight

My name is Mole.
I inhabit a hole
and pooter about in the dark.

I make my way
though earth and clay
under the lamb and the lark.

Tunnelling my run
far from the sun
I dig like a JCB.

I climb from my lair
and sniff the air –
tonight on BBC.

Rail crisis, a basically true story

From an incident recorded by D. Hickman in his
fascinating memoir 'Reminiscences of the Engineers'
Department, Southern Railway, Eastleigh.'

'There's a lady stuck in the loo
on Platform Two.'
That was the problem
on Southampton station
in late December '52.
What could they do?

What a shock to be stuck
in a station loo!
What terrible luck
as your train comes in
for Waterloo!

They phoned a message
along the line:
'We need a carpenter
urgently, a matu-
re chippy to free
a lady who
unfortunately
has got herself trapped
in the down-side loo
on Southampton Central
Platform 2.'

Up at Eastleigh
they heard the signal
relating the lady's
deep distress,
immediately stopped
the next express
and despatched a chippy
mature as Methu-
selah to assess
the scale of the problem
and see what to do.

The express steamed in
at Platform 2,
and along he came
stroking his chin
surveying the scene
maturely. He said:
'I can't unscrew
the seat from the pan
but what I can
attempt to do
is cut the bolts
then saw it in two;
I can't see anything
else to do
but cut off the bolts
and saw it in two,
yes that's what I'll do.'

And that's what he did.
While a lady attendant
concealed the patient
behind a tarpaulin,
he cut off the bolts
and started sawin-
g the seat in two,
keeping all the while
politely silent,
ladies being present,
one at the fundament
firmly incumbent.

Meanwhile outside
discussion continued:
'We can't leave this place
of frequent retreat
in deep mid-winter
without a seat
to repose the behind
on,' opined
the station-master
sternly, so

the carpenter's mate
– the not so mature one –
was sent on his bike
for another seat
and when he got back
with it round his neck
the old seat was off,

and the lady too
on the next train
to Waterloo,
after tipping them all
– the porters too –
for their promptitu-
ude and professional
skill in her rescue.

Meanwhile
the Railway, inclu
ding matu-
re and immatu-
re carpenters, expresses to
and from Waterloo
and the loo
itself on Platform 2
with its new
seat resu-
med service as normal.

Thinking things

Does that scaffolding
stand there thinking
without me perhaps
this bank will collapse?

Is that tractor
with arms held high
like a conductor
looking forward
to plunging them earthward?

As they blink,
do cameras think
that'll be
a lovely
or memorable
or quite nice sight –
if they got
film speed
focus
and light
right?

Promises

Leeks
the packet said.

I poured in the seed
and as suggested
waited

for two or three weeks.

Then there they were
sprouting in clouds
in their tray.

Thin them it said
and plant them out.

I obey.

They came on fast
over the next two weeks,
but the more they came on,
the more they weren't leeks.

It wasn't what
the packet said,
this cod crop of weeds
I'd planted tended grown
from leek seeds
tested and guaranteed.

The thing I forgot
was that I bought
only a rustling packet
of possibilities.

And what the chances are
of those producing the real thing,
whether it's leeks,
swedes, creeds,
parsnips, pensions, passions,

you only find out
when the future comes up
from under the promises.

Galileo's story

Galileo
Galilei
from Italy
invented seeing

a long way
and believing it.
He invented mountains
on the moon

and a lot of stars
that were further off
than the others.
He invented

leaning
over the leaning
tower of Pisa
saying *here's a*

big one coming down
and a little one
going the same speed
just you see.

He worked harder and harder
and got ill
so he invented
taking your temperature.

Before long
he'd invented
being right too often
when important

people were wrong
and had to invent
pretending to have
second thoughts

and important people
being right again.
His enemies'
only invention

was putting him
in prison
in his own home
when he was an old man

in case he did
any more damage
to their best
ancient ideas.

Frog at take-off

On wet grass
nib-faced
squat Concorde
up-angled
for take-off

ready to power
into the air
for the split-second
crossing
of the pond.

Noble poem of old, 'twill be

I've often tried to write a poem
with lots of **'twases** in it
and **'tweens** and **e'ens**, **enows** and **weens**
and **doths** and **don'ts** and **dursts** and **'twonts** –
but I've always had to bin it.

But today again I forge ahead –
a poem must get written
crammed to the brim with **thees** and **thous**
and agonising dying vows
and loving heroes smitten,
and doughty **damsels** clobbering knaves
and flaming dragons and spooks
and boring teachers chained in caves –
the lot of them, **gadsooks**!

It will not be a modern poem
there'll be no trains or buses
but blokes on **steeds** who when they bleeds
use **'zounds's** and **'sooths**
(not cors and 'struths)
and **'twas not erstwhile thuses**.

It will all occur
in days of **yore**
on yon far mountain's height
where cows are **kine**
and thou art mine
and heroes have to fight
dirty great huge grim bearded geezers
who block out all the light.

Forsooth egad, I **fain** would start!
What **dost thou**, reader, **thinkst**?
Trow'st it's a great idea?
Nay! Averrest thou
it stinkst?

Shield shape near twilight

Even staring for a minute at it
I can't work out what the light
is doing under the bridge.

The barrel of the arch underneath
and its curving edge seem furred
with the light of the setting sun

from behind the lit poplars beyond,
and then there's a faded shield
of more sun near me in the river itself.

I stare till I see it right. Crinkle
crankle the sun has come, tacking
at the speed of light, making

one, two, three diversions: first
off the river surface beyond
the bridge, then off its underside,

then off the water this side and up
to me: from water, stone, water,
to here. A mistle thrush distracts me,

three times crossing the river urgently
with his or her mouth full of stuff,
and by the time I turn back to the river

the moon is another faded shield
and the one the sun threw down has gone.
Unless it was no illusion but a true

shield let fall, and the hurt knight
of my imagination – who's long been lying
nearby in the shadows – has emerged

from the trees and hauled his dripping
arms from the river, and even now
begins to urge his mount away from here.

Perhaps that faint clop of hooves and clink
of bridle I can just hear from the road
beyond the darkened bridge is him.

Pies poem

In long-ago Lancashire
I can still see them –
all those pies

piled in little pyramids
at the back of steaming tea-stalls,
or sitting in misted-up shop windows.

All sorts of pies
in all sorts of places:

factory lunch-hour hot potato pies
that mill-girls queued for,
with a bit of hot meat floating about
and a lot of hot carrot;

artistic-looking beautifully carved proper pie-shop
                                            pies,
sitting between the sausages and the tripe and the
                                            trotters
in terraces and battlements and grottos
of pie on Thornleys' windows;

cricket-match tea-interval miniature pies;

pies crouched under glass bells in cafés
looking lonely;

little shrunk-inside
overdue railway-station pies;

big scalding watery pies
that we bought at Southport bus-station
to eat on the way home
on top of Oliver Hart's one and only
rackety old usually empty double-decker bus;

school tuck-shop pies
that you ate with Vimtos fizzing up your nose.

Good times for pies, were those.

Shepherd's crown

Shepherd's crown is the folk-name for a little
cone-shaped fossil, often found by the sea.
Its centre is flint, the outside is chalky
remains of a sea-urchin's shell from 70
million years ago or more.

Feet
walked it.

Death
emptied it.

Sea
took it.

Lives
filled it.

Oceans
lost it.

Aeons
gripped it.

A cliff
spilled it.

Beaches
rolled it.

Pebbles
scoured it.

Dawn
saw it.

We
rescue it.

The Aztec year of the warrior as the god 'Tezcatlipoca'

Already the flutes of the next god
moan softly in the streets
as high above in the sun
the heart steams its last in the eagle-dish,
the head is skewered on the skull rack.

Already another god has been found,
another captured warrior,
chosen for perfection of body,
for his unblemished limbs and skin.
Already he has been given the sacred clay flute.

We shall make him a great warrior,
we shall make him a lord and a god.
Motecuhzoma himself will bring him
capes of flowers, gold bells for his thighs,
sandals trimmed with the ears of the ocelot.

He will be taught to play the sacred flute
in the manner of a lord
and to carry a bouquet of flowers
and to hold the richly gilt tobacco tubes.

Warrior pages will go with him,
brilliant in cloaks with designs
of blue whirlpools and fishes,
shifting smoke, snakes, jaguars.
They will wear high waving headdresses
woven from the feathers
of brilliant red and yellow birds
and the rare green quetzal.

For the twenty days of Toxcatl
he will be married to four young maidens.

He will not hear the great bronze gong,
the two-toned boom of the serpent drum
as it greets the morning star.
He will forget the knives of the noon sun.

He will live content like a god
in the shade of poems and songs
in the shade of a dance
in the shade of a dream.

He will drink the torchlight and adulation.
He will bathe in pools of flowers.

The streets will greet him as if he were a king.
The waters will spread jade capes for him.
He will be praised and honoured.
He will believe his reign will last for ever.

So the god's year will go on
till the royal canoe carries him one morning
as the mists drift from the lake
as the volcanoes grow pale
to a small abandoned temple on the island
                                        shore.

There his wives will take leave of him,
the touch of their fingers will fall from him.
His numerous brilliant company
with the plumed headdresses will depart.
Their friendship will fade into the mist.

He will walk along the shore to the temple
playing the sacred clay flutes
which once he played
when he was a great lord and a god.

At the foot of the temple steps
his pages will turn aside.

He will raise his eyes to the sun
and climbing the temple
he will break at each step
one by one
the small clay flutes.

Looking only upwards
knowing now only the sun
its final knife of obsidian
he will ascend the few steps

to where the priests wait.

Saturday night seal

In Falmouth harbour
something going

smoothly through chip-wrappings
something like a shoulder

black as an old inner tube
glistening disappears

then after a minute
juts up

twirling seal whiskers
snuffling like a cross old major

as he looks towards the shops
from under his eyebrows' pale

little plastic aerials
and swivels

towards the watchers
who wonder who he's looking for

on Saturday at 7 pm
as the grey eyes

swoon down again
then half a minute

later twenty feet
away rise

to greet some kind
of keeper who's come

dangling keys
of fish.

House

In the morning this house
has two sunlit bays
watching it.
Boats from Italy

throb by slowly.
In the garden's shade
glow oranges.
Through the dead hot noon

cypresses guard
its iron gates
while the eucalyptus
whispers its secrets.

Some afternoons
thunder sails low
dripping dark
from torn sides of cloud,

or its sky of birds
spins frantic
as a falcon falls.
In the evening swallows

hurtling through
examine its rooms.
A lamp burns.
We read, open

some wine, eat,
watch the moon
rise, wait
for the owl's call.

What you do with a storm

in a Greek street at 7 o'clock
is buy an umbrella in its honour
and stand there

watching

a man with an umbrella
meeting a priest without one
for a long talk

two girls catching dribbles
from the telephone wires
in a empty crisp-bag

customers asking the waiter
can he stop it streaming
through the flapping awning

the waiter moving tables inside
while another watches it waterfalling
down the swinging light-fitting

dark clouds bumping into each other
on thundery manoeuvres out at sea
the headland coming into sight again

and the island reappearing
then as the sun comes out
someone finding an abandoned

umbrella.

Hell's off – Parga, NW Greece

DAY TRIP TO HADES!
but not today.

'Yes, 'e is not today,
the water 'es bouncing,

head hit roof in cave,
is dangerous.

See river come out
yes not go in,

too dangerous,
no Styx, not possible.

Safe tomorrow,
better tomorrow!

Go to 'ades tomorrow!'

Roman terror

An hour from Hardknott Fort's grim walls
high on icy Lakeland fells

my mind still full of England full of Romans,
their British slaves and Welsh silver,

gladiators dying at Colchester,
mosaics with sea-leopards and dolphins

sporting far away to the south at Bignor
where they lived near where I live,

feeling the presence in places I drive through
of Roman soldiers – marching, repairing bridges,

galloping with the Imperial post,
sprawled at the road's edge for a rest,

loading carts, digging camps.
Driving into twilight

along a stretch of old Roman road
and slowing down through the woods

something pulled my head round
to glance out. He'd already

pulled level with the car –
a Roman charioteer

overtaking me, whipping
his horses frantically, going flat out.

He glanced in at me, then back ahead,
white knuckles clenching reins,

a sweat-soaked forehead,
sun glinting on shoulder armour,

chariot wheels that bounced
and leapt, hurling up dust and gravel.

I slammed to a stop, clenching the wheel.
He swerved in front of me, slewing across

so a wheel ran for a second at the edge
of the ditch, then he recovered

and disappeared round the bend,
with just one terrified glance back.

After my moment of panic I started again,
foot hard down to catch him.

The road was empty for miles.
Woodland peace and calm,

no ancient or modern vehicles.
No charioteer, no marching legionaries.

No more chilling glances across the centuries.
Only dust still hanging faintly

under miles of beeches.

Talking pet-shop owner

'Now that quail
you could take today,
or the barn-owl on the rail,

or any kind of parrot
you want. On special
offer this week we've got

a cuddly pair
of marmoset monkeys.
Somewhere in there

you should be able to see
our deadly tropical spider.
Or perhaps you'd prefer

a genuine bird of prey –
this young kestrel was hatched
on the twentieth of May.

The way that monkey hammers
his paws along the bars!
No, he's not for sale,

he's a pet already.
But that quail,
or the barn-owl on the rail . . .'

When the Creator made the birds

He gave each of them their uses

Blackbird
to dig with a sharp beak
and find gold song

        Heron
        to move to murder
        on slow
        theatrical
        tip-toe

                Woodpecker
                to beat his brain on beech
                a thousand times an hour

        Coot
        to go nod nod nodding
        a white-shielded head
        at nothing nothing nothing

    Gull
    to be the seaside's shrill
    town-crier

Pigeon
to sit cor-ing and cooing
you-hey-you-ing
anything doing?

Redshank
to go echo-sounding
in estuary shallows

     Duck
     to be teacher
     of waddling and rude laughter

    Dunlin
    to prod wet mud in hundreds
    rise and shimmer as one

Nightjar
to drill for music
in the silent craters
of the June moon

Owl
to speak of death
and ghostly things

    Kestrel
    to hang and turn in the wind
    winter and summer

        Buzzard
        to trail the coat of his shadow
        over the lamb

  Wren
  to sing hours
  of atom-rapid micro-music a minute

Thrush
to break open the shell
where light lies

Robin
to be a singing small fire
in the tree's quiet rain

Kingfisher
to hurl along shaded waters
a burning atom of sun

Lark
to build skies on earth

Grebe
to be the pond's
resident
mad professor

Swallow
to embroider a summer for us
and strew our paths
with rumours of winter

Scientists all together now making a new animal exactly the same

It's a breakthrough in technology.
We've achieved a technological breakthrough.
It's a radical technological advance.
We've performed a technological breakthrough.
It's a great technological leap forward.

Definitely. We're in total agreement.

Shall we call her Dolly?
Perhaps Dolly would be a good name?
I think Dolly's the right one personally.
Would Dolly sound right?
Why not Dolly?
I suggest Dolly.
Does Dolly fit?

Let's vote. We're in total agreement.

We could do the same with humans.
It would work with humans.
We could do the same thing with the human species.
It's technologically possible to produce identical humans.
We could make humans the same as each other.

So we all agree? In theory. Yes.

But we wouldn't want to make humans into clones.
But it wouldn't be right having people thinking
                    the same thoughts.
But we wouldn't want to hear people saying
                    the same things.

It wouldn't be practicable, having hundreds of them
                    called Jim,
Or Jim,
Or Jim,
Or Jim,
Or Jim.

I mean would it?
I mean would it?
I mean would it?
I mean would it?

People are different, you see.
People are different, you see.
People are different, you see.
People are different, you see.

Accidental proverbs

It takes two to flog a dead horse.

Still waters come but once a year.

Rats run deep.

When in doubt, desert a sinking ship.

Revenge wasn't built in a day.

A contented mind must be endured.

Don't cut off your nose in mid-stream.

Gather ye rosebuds where credit is due.

Curiosity is mightier than the sword.

Seeing is blind.

Ignorance killed the cat.

Absence is the best sauce.

Love is the mother of invention.

Necessity springs eternal.

Travel broadens the mouth.

Look before you grow fonder.

Odin, god of poetry and wisdom

To get poetry, Odin snaked deep
into the mountain and stole it from giants.
To get wisdom, he gave away an eye,

threw one eye in the old pool
that suddenly seethed,
then he hung for seven days near death

on the knowledge tree, Yggdrasill,
riding the horse of its gallows
till he came to know what the dead know,

came to know spells to scatter sky-hags,
spells to turn the flight of a spear with his eye,
to calm the sea and hold the gale still.

Now he discovers
in the hiss of lava spattering on glaciers
more than we'll ever know.

He has only to part curtains of flame
to hear the roar of the future.
If the war's uncertain

he consults a skirmish of ice-floes,
in peace reads what the air's hand
writes on the still lake.

Throned where his ravens cry
he sees past, present, future, hears
the wren's shell breaking open,

scents what the sleek-headed otter
nosing upriver scents along its gravels.
When he learns what's to be,

when he's heard under ice the long
song of the whales,
and gathered from cliffs of snow

the fish-eagle's scream,
he works his words on the wind's ringing
anvils, inscribes runes, stains them

with sun, lightning, shadow, hammering
from hail and snow
a hoard of songs, hymns

of the world, its first things, endings,
gleaming eagle eggs, the osprey's
fall, scarves of flowers at the fjord's brim.

Dear problem page

I'm writing about this temptation I get.

Sometimes when I go for a walk
on the hill in autumn
I think how enjoyable it would be
to start rolling downhill one or two
of those round Rolo-shaped bales
they leave all over the hillside
at all angles and inclinations
glistening invitingly in the sun
and wanting to be rolled gently downhill
just longing for a little shove.

The farmers shouldn't leave them there,
waiting so temptingly . . .
It makes you wonder
whether some of them ever roll down on their own,
or if you have to push hard.

You imagine the noise they make on the stubble,
and what it would be like watching one get going,
would it stop after a few feet
or keep on bumping and skipping down
at about the same pace to the bottom;

perhaps it might do a jog
and alter course unexpectedly and go trundling
down through the gate across the road
or maybe it would keep going straight down
in the same direction you aimed it
till it comes come to a gentle standstill
with a lovely swish in the hedge.

As I say I get this temptation sometimes,
up it starts like a lark.
I even hope I might see someone
pushing at a bale or two
testing for wobbliness
till they find a good rocky one
look round for a second
and give it a good firm
        push

just to see . . . what happens . . .
I wonder what would happen.

A friend of mine once gave into this temptation.
I know him quite well.

Road to the beach

Where the road peters out past Atherington Villas
the beach begins, with concrete blocks
left over from the war.

At the edge of the water
my tyres make a gentle hiss on the sand.

The tide's far out.
It's quiet. Whoever left behind
these perfect young small footprints
that make the sand paler
and the kids who performed
perfect wheelies and elaborate 8s
have gone home for tea.

Avoiding shredded tyres of sea-wrack
and mounds of dead cuttle-fish,
swinging round to ride west
I face a shine of sun
on wet sand, long gleaming
plates of beach rivetted
with thousands of worm-casts.

A surf-board glints
as it walks itself free of sea glitter.
In the heat-shimmer
a large person divides
to a couple ending an embrace.

Things aren't what they seem.

Wheels splash through water
where the beach drains
in tiny rivers over sand
sculpted to woven sinew and muscle
like exposed tissue
in a medical diagram.

Dawdling through pools
at the tide's still edge,
seeing things
only the lowest tides of the year
pull back to uncover,
when green-weeded stones
send my wheels joddering
this way and that
I dismount,

and it's then I realise
searching down hard
in a rock pool's
lower sky of blue,
seeing scattered brick
worn and broken,
I'm standing in
vanished Atherington.

From there too
one could wander out
to the tide's far edge and find
smudge-marks of romping dogs,
tracks of hooves and cart-wheels,
the perfect young small footprints
of children who ran home for tea
thousands of tides ago.

Paris 1950 – Avenue Simon Bolivar, by Willy Ronis

It's early, with no flowers or leaves out yet,
in Paris in a wintry spring. A photograph

of a flight of steps and railings down to a road,
then railings dropping out of sight beyond.

Long shadows of bare trees and lamp-posts,
a horse and cart and a set of traffic lights,

tangle across the sunlit road and pavement.
Thirteen lives inhabit the picture, if you count

a cat peeking from behind a low stone wall
and the blinkered horse hauling a two-wheeled cart

that carries an old man huddled into his coat
holding the reins from a seat on empty boards.

On the bottom step the left foot of the woman
holding a child on her arm is about to step

on her left foot's shadow. The baby in a pram
on the far pavement turns sideways to stare

at the great big horse pulling the great big cart.
The sun as it touches the downward arc of the reins

makes it seem they're attached not to the horse
but the two-woman team chatting and pushing the pram –

unless one's doing the pushing and one the talking.
How true it seems, this ordinary busy moment

when thirteen lives paused on the way to somewhere
fifty years ago in Paris, in March perhaps, observed

in black and white from the top of a flight of steps.
A man in a white overall guards his shop,

watching a woman walking by with a push-chair
for the boy holding her hand or perhaps the shopping

to ride in later. The bike leaning on the railings with a coat
wrapped round the crossbar belongs to the workman

reaching up from a trestle ladder to change
a pedestrian traffic-light bulb, or perhaps clean it.

The metal studs on the crossing gleam from shadow,
the sun stresses the design of manhole covers,

the circular grilles guarding the base of trees,
the pavement's patched bits, and the road's stone setts,

laid – so horses won't slip – the way a tide
shapes sand into overlapping crescents sometimes.

And here in my room the horse goes plodding on
down the same street to nowhere, past children

who never yet said a word. The two women
haven't got on with their shopping,

the trees haven't found time to break into leaf,
the foot waits as patiently over its shadow.

Of course. It's only a picture, of a single moment,
and things don't alter in pictures. Except that this

is so full of life passing by and just passing,
the instant would have gone beyond remembering

if the camera hadn't held it in mid-moment,
stopped these people going on their way

to show us what we are doing, at its simplest,
when the only thing happening is simply being alive.

Purrson to person

I have just come in from **purrsuing** things in the garden

       where a **purrfidious** mouse ran away from me
and an **impurrtinent** robin
not appreciating my **purrsonality**

       Purradventure it's time for tea?

How **purrplexing**
I think you know **purrfectly** well it's teatime
I shall **purrsevere**
I scent **purrfume** of fish

Mm I'mmm a hundred **purrcent** correct again of course

More **purrhaps**?
fish is one of my **purrquisites**
and that was all a bit **purrfunctory**
though nothing's **purrmanent** I suppose

You can **purrsuade me** off the table
but I don't need **purrmission** to lie here
when necessary I'm **impurrturbable**

No I don't want to be **purrpetually** picked up
sometimes you're not a very **purrspicacious**
purrson are you?

thankyou I'm **purrfectly** content here
purrusing the garden

except

might you **purrchance** be lighting the fire soon?

Cat,

now you've abandoned
every last shopping basket
waste-bin and tool box

and aren't to be discovered
drowsing guilty-eyed
in the airing cupboard;

now you no longer
whisk over the grass
preparing superfine leaps

at nothing, and aren't
roused by the taunts
of a single leaf's

scampering,
it's as if
you decided to leave

all that to next door's
young cat;
us slowly

to get used
to not seeing you
raise intense claws

to the apple trees
in daily praise
of blossom and leaf,

not watching you
turn to watch us –
where now we observe

only grief.

Where have the paths gone? –
The devil's taken them.

Tobacco ready for picking,
sugarcane tall in the fields.
Sun rose, tapped the blinds.
'Dreaming's done, get going.'

But no one walks the road to the fields,
no one goes on the paths.
There are no paths, no roads,
they're lost, gone away somewhere,
high grass and forest have taken them in the night.

No roads, paths. No one goes anywhere.
No one goes working the fields.
No one visits friends or family.
People stay home, longing for sea-sounds,
for the high cool mountain.
Can't go looking for lost children, lost family.

Weary, weary, weary.
Stone bored. Tired not doing anything.
No plans, hopes, all gone down the lost paths.
No dreams, all swallowed up.
No tobacco, no sugarcane.
Hot, dusty, dead, choked up, tumbledown old world.

The devil has taken the paths and roads.
It's old choke-road strangle-path Okurri Boroku,
Okurri Boroku has taken the paths, the roads,
given them to the high grass and the trees.

The people hopeless for years and years
in their bad dream of an island.

Then a thing happened that had hope in it:
twins were born to an old couple,
hero magic twins, ibelles – magic-makers
with the tremble of magic light round them.

Taewo and Kainde grew up quickly.
They had fun being twins,
fooling their friends and teachers
who was who,
changing places with each other
fooling, the way twins do.
But they grew up quickly in their minds
and saw how people lived
in a dead old place, in a dead old time.
They knew they had to leave
to find Okurri Boroku and kill him.

Magically fading through the high grasses and forest
they wandered and wandered the island looking.

For seven months, nothing, nothing,
then a cool morning, a sandy beach by the sea,
a pile of driftwood, and another,
for a fire.

Nearer they came. Driftwood –
and bones! Folks' bones! Bones of folks
Okurri trapped on choked-up gone roads!

Okurri Boroku is somewhere near!
Too near! Listen! They heard him,
louder than the sea, louder than the sea in the palms,
Okurri Boroku snoring,
and they went to the edge of the forest and looked in
at a stretched out pile of ugly devil sleeping.
Sagged-open poison-flower mouth, curved yellow teeth
like bananas, hair choked with seeds and feathers.

The twins knew what they had to do,
after they had woken him.

But they couldn't wake him.
They shook him and beat him with sticks,
threw water on him, shouted terrible
insults in his ears but he wouldn't wake.
Then they wafted some petals of fragrant frangipani
in his nostrils and the smell troubled him and began
                            to wake him.

It was time for Kainde to fade into the bushes.

Okurri saw Taewo. Laughed – what was so funny? –
making all the beach birds flap off.
'My breakfast lighting the fire for my breakfast!'
was what was funny.

Taewo acted. *'Oh please, Okurri Boroku,*
make me some big high challenge, please,
to give me a chance to win escape
from quick breakfast. And I tell the world
what a fine monster devil old Okurri Boroku
really is.'

Okurri looked at him, suspicious,
then suddenly grinned
and grabbed an old leather case,
and the sun off the water reflected
on a shiny black guitar.

'You play and I dance? OK?
You play the devil guitar, make him
dance to your tune,
keep me dancing to your tunes.
Keep playing, playing, playing.
Till the sun set, then rise, then
go down again. Till you drop,
or Okurri Boroku drop.'
He threw back his head and laughed,
and the cliffs laughed back and the birds
took off again scrawking.

Taewo started playing
the wildest fastest tune he knew,
and the old devil danced and danced
like a twelve year-old. He stamped
and swayed and his hands went weaving
the air and his head beat and rhythmed it
till the valley shook and reeled round,
and on and on it went for hours with Okurri
hammering the sand with his eyes closed
and Taewo's hands flying on the silver strings.

The Taewo stopped and said, *'I'm thirsty sir,*
can I drink at the stream quickly?'
Okurri wanted a quick rest,
so he said 'OK', and Taewo slipped into the bushes
and handed the guitar to Kainde, and Kainde's
fresh fingers and hands turned up the beat
and the pace got so wild and hot that Okurri Boroku
poured sweat and more sweat and his hair
started to smoke and spurts of steam came
whistling out from his ears like from under panlids.
He was breathing fast but he shouted *'Good rhythms!*
Hot fast breakfast music! You beaten yet? Play,
boy, play! Keep that old black guitar sound flying!'

'I need another quick drink at the stream sir first,'
Kainde said, and Okurri took a short breather
while Kainde slipped the guitar back to Taewo
fooling Okurri again like they used to fool their friends
and then Taewo drove the pace up again faster than ever.

And now as the devil danced to Taewo's tune
his body was humming like some electric machine
and sparks started to fly off his shoulders and hands
and flickered along his teeth and fizzed out of
                                his nostrils.

And they stopped for another drink at the stream
                                in the bushes.

And Kainde took over
crowding the thumping beats
out of that shiny old black guitar
till it got hot strings
and Okurri's thick
dirty old hair went on end
like a jelly-fish,

then Taewo again
and the moon came up
and bats came down
jinking round
and owls hooted
then the pile of old bones
started to stir
and bones got to their feet
and started creaking and clinking
and jittering round in the moonlight,
tippling and jangling into each other –
they were out of practice dancing –
till at midnight the whole valley
was blue with leaping bones.

And the moon was full on the water
and Okurri Boroku was nearly finished
with his forked blue tongue hanging out
from a sicky yellow devil-grin,
and his body going slower and slower,
his devil-scales creaking
his red eyes bulging
as he slowly leaned and toppled
and with the noise of ten houses collapsing
he slumped and fell.

And that was the end
of choke-road Okurri Boroku, and the end
of the dead trapped time on the island.
Since then, hopes and desires travel freely,
and when the guitar sings at night
the paths remember.

Tobacco ready for picking.
Sugarcane tall in the fields.
Sun rises, taps the blinds.
'Dreaming's done. Get going.'

And folks walk the roads to the fields.

And at night when the guitar sings
the paths themselves remember.

Hedghog and moonlight

Out from under
shrubs and plants

for a moonlight potter
that's mainly blunder

sniffs and grunts,
starting his half-hour

stroll with a trundle
round the dustbin,

busy legs doing
a rapid crossing

of moonlit yard
and whispering gravel,

then wavering across
the grass towards supper

in wait at the white tin
plate of milky

bread he treads in
nightly till quietly

the moon goes in
while clinking

sounds of feeding
still fill the garden.

Gliders

The behaviour
of these geometrical
birds is ceremonious –
with what civilised
demeanour they
meet each other,
gravely dipping
a fin in greeting,
turning slowly
to rinse a wing
of shadow or un-
sleeve it of sun.

Sea view

At its terminus by the sea
this old carriage stopped

rolling no longer
stock stationary

and only the wind has whistled
the flying sand through

and only flowers
have tapped the wheels

since the time when the wheels
lost their song to the gulls

and time got out
and made net curtains

of the waves.

On television tonight

And now the desert runs
in leaps and bounds
over the plains

and overtakes the ox
who's famished
and slow

and has too many ribs
and nowhere to go.

The ox is slow and sinks to its knees.

The river got tired long ago.

The desert with its hungry stride
gains ground
on people
who've forgotten
where green has gone.

Tonight the desert wins.

On millions of screens
we follow the losers
trailing nowhere
in never-ending columns
so many mothers
whose breasts are empty rivers
so many children
with arms as thin as a whisper.

Then the ads break in to say
        look at the scrumptious goo
queuing up for you,
        have a nice day
look the other way.

But we've just seen
a different screen

and heard it scream.

As, as, as . . .

As slow as a start
as stopped as a heart
as thin as a chip
as chapped as a lip
as dour as a door
as high as the floor
as far as away
as near as today
as dreamy as far
as tall as a star
as dark as a lock
as stopped as a clock
as slow as a hiss
as near as a miss

as slim as an 'i'
as puzzled as 'y'
as warm as a purr
as boring as sir
as boring as sir
as boring as sir
as scrunched as a list
as white as a fist .
as bold as a blizzard
as old as a wizard
as sad as the sea
as fit as a flea
as sick as our cat
as yukky as that
as slow as an end
as there as a friend
as quick as a kiss
as finished as this.

Gold rush – how to get rich
by reading history

You could try one of the ways of getting rich
the Greek historian, Herodotus, describes.
He says a one-eyed people, the Arimaspi,
simply steal gold from griffins.
(First find your griffins.)
A second way he describes sounds more possible.
He says a certain Persian people
accumulate great hoards of gold
by training desert creatures to find it for them.
These Persian people – he says –
told him that in the desert live huge ants
'bigger than foxes', who are always digging up sand,
and the sand the ants dig up – nearly non-stop –
has gold in it. So the hunters of desert gold
harness three camels – two male and one female –
and ride out at the hottest time of the day,
and while the ants take their underground siestas,
leaving the gold-filled sand they've dug up
in piles unguarded, the Persian hunters, if
they're luckily uninterrupted,
fill bag after bag with sand that's full of gold.
It's a rush, because as soon as the ants
smell them or their camels – or just something
fishy – they scramble from their underground shelters
and give chase. Across the desert in clouds of dust
the camels go charging home with a pack of huge ants
snapping their mad antennae at their heels.

Sometimes the slower camels – the males –
get caught and killed. The females –
                        who are faster because
(according to the Persian version) they're thinking
all the time about their offspring –
usually get back safely with their riders.
Herodotus says these people also say, by the way,
some captured ants are kept
at the palace of the Persian king.
Which is also quite interesting.

Newt

I own dragons.
One of them hangs
in the pond this morning

drowsing, hand-like feet spread
in free fall. He slews
a few degrees,

swaying the way
a boat I remember
at anchor in Loggos harbour

in sunlit water
swayed, with the hive-shaped
cloud of fry

under it – the way an eyes-
closed gold-bellied
tiny marine

dragon sways
in amber sun dreaming.
Neither grass-blade nor leaf

pushed gently
arouses him, but when
an iris stem

tips him
a millimetre or so over
he plunges

a balancing
hand down
for a firmer hold

on his dream.

The Emperor Nero

Nero?
No hero –
definitely not.
Short, squat
malodorous,
says Suetonius.
Features, pretty –
not witty.
Legs, spindling –
mind, dwindling.
Unmuscular,
pustular.
One of history's
nastier little mysteries.
Takes life
of one wife
then another
plus aunt, mother,
step-brother and step-son
(for playing with emperor clothes on).
Strums his lyre
while Rome's on fire –
the Imperial twit
probably started it
to make building space

for another mile of palace;
blames Christians,
sews them in animal skins
for dogs to tear to bits.
Adores the glitz
of the stage.
Takes an age
to do his act –
'half-cracked',
they say but while he's on
no one
leaves, so old men
get coronaries and women
have babies or act dead
to get carried
out. Athletics
next – the Olympics;
flattened in the ring,
and in his charioteering
debut thrown clean out
of the chariot –
to thunderous applause
and another first prize.
Suicide at thirty-two.
All too true.

Ebernoe grass snake

Ebernoe is a tract of ancient woodland in Sussex.

A lisp
underfoot

cruises away
under the beeches

signing itself
in Ss

trailing
a wake of itself

the prow
of its head lifted

clear above waves
of last year's leaves.

Froglet

Here

comes a
tenth-size
froglet

plink
plink
plink

leaping
over
endless

grass
like a let-out
tiddly

wink

Moon, frost, deer

Lengthening clear
of hedge-shadow

shadows of deer
on the field's frost-

white mooon-sheer
stubble floor, crisp-

footed through the swung-
open metal barred gate

into the lane to wait
nudging each other,

restlessly still,
a small noisy silence

of collaborating breath
till a tremor sends

them, hooves
skidding gently, off

down the stiff white path
trailing mist-warmth.

4.40 pm, November

A red bike
wrenched concave.

A white face
shielded by

a whitely thin
arm. A van

on its side in
muddied grass.

Glistening
frost, glass.

Headgear
they all

have on.
Anyone's

son.

Deer's skull

This awkward chalky latch
must have been what flicked the ears
this way and that,

and this snapped biro-end of bone
the thin corridor
that sounds of the fields crowded down.

To think these dusty caves of muzzle
were once aswirl
with the woods' faint scents,

and that under this brain's thin
meander of suture, suns rose
and stars fell.

I wonder when it last stared
across the hot whisper of this wheatfield
watching someone watching.

Hunting in February

I'm hunting this morning
with the eye and the ear
not the gun.
I'm out to catch the sun

in icy ditches.
I'm tracking two nuthatches
avoiding me
tree after tree.

I peer in each pond,
scan each path
for signs
of wakening earth.

I watch on a fence-post
a dozing hawk
ignoring a crow's
scold and scrawk,

hear frogs creak
their old hosannas
from the melting pond's
slimy saunas,

catch a glimpse
at the Rother's edge
of grayling sunning
under Shopham bridge.

Eye and ear
are the gear to use
for throwing over creatures
the mind's noose.

You'll only ever
hold in the heart's
keepnet the glitter
of sudden kingfisher,

or the clear glance
the fox gives you
paused at the lane's
edge in rain;

You need no weapon
to bag a fine pheasant
or stalk the heron
at the pond's rim,

or snare the shadows
clouds pull
across the fields
under Duncton Hill.

Ebernoe nightingale

Live
in concert

a shepherd's whistlings slow
as clouds on the fell

seconds of low
mellow drill

bursts of revving
amplified wren

a large slow wheel turning
on a titanium axle

a hawser straining musically

a steady contralto
slow-motion bee

a minute's meltdown to
pure silver

ricochets round a canyon
in a Western

silence
the slow huge wheel again

Crossing the airfield

The musical growl of an old Spitfire
fills the air here

all morning. Up from Goodwood
people on expensive trips

to the past, reliving the war perhaps.
The day when the Stukas

fell on Ford, unprepared.
From Ford and Tangmere

they scrambled, took to the air
in minutes, fanned out

over the Channel, up screaming
into the sun, up from this old concrete

runway that's still in good order.
Crossing it on the bike,

tyres humming past turnings
to what were the hangars,

faster and faster
down the middle of the runway

till the tyres' hum lifts to a whine,
the concrete racing underneath,

and suddenly it seems as if
I might be one of those taking off

and might not be coming back.

Mr Waters, agent, sells nearly anything nearly anywhere

My thanks to Derrick Palengat, the owner of the book,
for the opportunity to study it and make use of it here.

No brochures in those days.
1856, 1849, 1866 are three of the dates
in Mr Waters' book of drawings of samples
of locomotives, cranes, houses for emigrants,
toolsheds, ploughs, wheelbarrows, boilers for boats –
nearly anything useful nearly anywhere in the Empire.

Measuring over two feet from top to bottom,
20 inches across, weight about 25 lbs,
in places falling to bits, page-edges near to ash –
you wonder how many years it took
to gather it all together. And how did he manage
to lug it from harbour to station to hotel,
across plains to dusty nowheres, up dizzy tracks
to soaking mountain towns slumped under clouds?
He did it somehow. He and his great book
took steamer out from England several times
and travelled Australia, Canada, Nigeria,
Singapore, Borneo, and it's anyone's guess where else.

A hundred and fifty years ago, an agent
to buy from, Mr Waters.
No ordering direct either,
behind his back, from the maker –
the manufacturers' names are all scratched out.

In Valparaiso or Cape Town or Sydney,
he was your man for railways;
Mr Waters undertook undamaged delivery
of the 'Prince Arthur Engine' [interior view
in colour, with flames], and the sturdy '1849
Tank Engine' [fire-box 2' 11" by 3' 6"], as well as
accessories like 'Railings Suitable
for Approaches to Railway Stations' [9s 6d
a section], and the probably very necessary
'Rail Straightening Machine'.

You can almost hear him: *'As for carriages, sir,*
all at 10% off for a limited period.
I do a fine 1st class at £376, 2nd at £250,
and 3rd – wood seats, no lighting – at £210.
Replacement wheels with axle, £18 the set,
two wheels, yes, fine bargains, sir,
and I shan't be out here again, sir, for some years.'

I wonder how many 'Emigrants' Iron Hut',
with 'Emigrants' Waggon' and 'Gentlemen's Tool chest
No 6' Mr Waters' persuasive sales-pitch set up
on the plains of South Africa or the Canadian mid-West.

Did he ride the thousand-mile Congo and the Niger
as well as the rivers of New South Wales
(with this folded map) selling his 'Oscillating
Marine Engines with Feathering Paddles'
and the 'Boiler as for SS Rainbow'?
I wonder how many shining boilers he sold
and how many blew up.

Then when the settlers settled and grew their gardens
how many thoughtful husbands at his suggestion
bought their wives 'The Improved Portable Brass
Garden Engine – Adapted for Lady Gardeners'?
How many pioneer bathrooms featured his 'Original
Bidet with Revolving Spray and Foot-pump'?

A book full of necessary ordinary things, a portrait
of Mr Waters building an empire of usefulness.
And a strange book too, with its mysterious
immaculately drawn 'Tin Oil Valencers',
and 'Chilled Iron Wheels Hooped at Naves'.

But the real mysteries are deeper, not written down
or beautifully traced, or artistically colour-washed,
or painstakingly highlighted like the shine
                        on brass wheel-hubs.
How did he survive three years of Borneo, the
                        humid heat
and fierce storms, the high trails churned to mud?
How did he actually do his work?
Did he lash his book to a mule to ride twenty miles
through tropical downpours to uncertain buyers waiting
in insectile dark at the back of some stinking nowhere?
Did locals sit all night in dim hotels
by the light of a pair of oil-lamps watching him
as his finger moved to interpret
the great painted book,
conjuring a brightly mechanised future
for themselves and their children, till they dreamed
high pressure beam engines and patent gold washers,
turntables, crushing machines, travelling cranes
swivel cranes and brick and tile machines
worked by animal or engine power at 37 rpm?
Did someone ask *Is 37*
a western magic number? Did the customer
drink just the right amount too much
deciding he needed a Planing, Moulding, Mortising,
Tennoning and Boring machine?

So many questions. Supposing he'd lost his book?
Did anyone ever try to steal it?
Did the promised goods always turn up?
Did he ever get lost or ill in a place on no map?
How many dreamed-of futures ever happened?
And where are all the fine things
of iron and brass now?
Where are the small wharf cranes,
the gleaming 1st class carriages,
the shingling hatchets and Kentucky wedge axes,
the hydraulic presses for crushing groundnuts?
I imagine the harrows, ploughs, carts, stoves
slumped half out of sight round delapidated farmyards,
the hulks of SS Rainbow and foundered others
listing up to their rails in river-mud,
the beautiful blue-bright tank engines
stretched on their sides in abandoned sugar-plantations,
or standing in sheds of forest that hide old sidings,
sturdy enough to steam huffily out again sometime
though now their fire-grates are home
to creatures who stay near home –

as for the rest, whose guess?

And the family in England, whenever did they see him?

Old navigation, Shopham

Puzzling to find it
in the middle of countryside
at its Sussex laziest
and summeriest nowhere,
this few hundred yards bit
of Industrial Revolution –
a straight navigation cut
along a mall of oak and alder.

At one end there's a ruined lock
with the brickwork coming apart,
and only a bit of timber
left of one of the gates
that last swung open
perhaps a hunded and fifty years ago
to let the last wooden barge
perhaps carrying coal
up towards Midhurst wharf.

It's the watery noise from the alders' shade
on the other side of the cracked brick bridge
that puzzles you. You go over the bridge
and push crouching through under oak branches
to find narrow walls
with fern and saplings sprouting from each side,
and over the basin's broken ledge
the outflow performing a minor waterfall
to rejoin the river
that's been on an aimless wander
through a field of cows.

Sprawl long enough here
of a late summer afternoon
watching the untroubled river
and the untroubled cows grazing,
listen hard enough into the alders
and you'll start to hear
the timber creak
of gates being hauled open;
a barge slews to midstream,
a dripping rope tautens,
men mop sweat from brows
and pause to measure the hills
with a slow eye.

They knew the river
in deep winter too,
banks turned white
and the locks frozen over;
they knew the intent near-quiet
of the valley in spring or Autumn flood,
whole fields in spate, river-banks
giving in without warning;
they knew its deaths and dramas,
the barn and farm burning,
a child's drowning.

But the old canal ghosts come closest
in September afternoons'
hazy silences,
like today, at a moment
like now, when you hear
in a pigeon's voice somewhere,
ambiguous in the mist,
the slow-paced
winding of an old hoist.

Stargrazer

When you're fourteen or fifteen
swinging up at the stars
is no problem
clamped in a cage on the arm
of a vertical carousel
to the throb of starry music
turning over and over
on a thing like a windmill blade
revolving faster then slower
as the beat thickens

Your shrieks
at fourteen don't mean anything
It's just fun
to look at the moon
upside down
from inside your cage while it hangs there
opposite the other upside-down cage
facing the other way
laughing, waiting, hanging there
feet up to the stars

Then you swing down
past the town's lights and lit roads
with cars and the houses beyond
and surge up again
all the light smearing down
past you as you climb to the ceiling of stars
and hang there again waiting
the guitars throbbing

Then the great yellow arms
start to loop you over and over
faster and faster
the air whooshing past
as if you were in an old plane
looping the loop
every light and star a blur
as you hurl towards earth
and skim the up-turned faces
and go soaring again
and straight over at the top
passing the other cage
like two planes just missing
whooshing over and whooshing over
till you close your eyes
pretending you're nowhere
trying to ignore the see-saw
blood flooding down to your head
up to your feet your head your feet

And it goes on a bit too long
but finally the lights go from blur
to whirl to just being there

And you aren't dizzy
and the shrieks are only pretend
or pretend they're pretend
and there are only a few more swings
over and over
faster then pause
then slower then faster
then longer pause

And you're not panicky you're ok
upside down at the top
with your clothes falling round you
and money falling in your pockets
and the blood falling to your head
as you look at the moon down there under your feet
and the fair and the town up there
or across at the cage full of funny-looking
upside-down kids looking at you
who might be the friends you'll see soon
the right way up
when you get down

As on the next turn down you finally do
and Stargrazer rocks to rest
as the beat slows
and the assistant opens the gates

and you're fourteen and run and hug your friends
and say it was marvellous I was terrified not really
or you leap down over the railings
and make a springy landing from eight feet

and grandad can't believe any of it.